AMAZING MYSTERIES

VAMPIRES

BY ASHLEY GISH

CREATIVE EDUCATION • CREATIVE PAPERBACKS

Published by Creative Education and Creative Paperbacks
P.O. Box 227, Mankato, Minnesota 56002
Creative Education and Creative Paperbacks are imprints of
The Creative Company
www.thecreativecompany.us

Design by The Design Lab
Production by Dana Koehler
Art direction by Rita Marshall
Printed in the United States of America

Photographs by Alamy (Chronicle, markku murto/art, World History
Archive), Dreamstime (Birica Eugen), Getty Images (Noam Galai/
FilmMagic), iStockphoto (Renphoto, tenra, Vladimir Zapletin,
Zeferli), Shutterstock (Bennyartist, Fablok, LaineN), SuperStock
(Stock Connection)

Library of Congress Cataloging-in-Publication Data
Names: Gish, Ashley, author.
Title: Vampires / Ashley Gish.
Series: Amazing mysteries.
Includes index.
Summary: A basic exploration of the appearance, behaviors, and
origins of vampires, the nocturnal mythological creatures known
for drinking blood. Also included is a story from folklore about a
vampire-hunting dhampir.
Identifiers:
ISBN 978-1-64026-221-8 (hardcover)
ISBN 978-1-62832-784-7 (pbk)
ISBN 978-1-64000-356-9 (eBook)
This title has been submitted for CIP processing under LCCN
2019937873.

First Edition HC 9 8 7 6 5 4 3 2 1
First Edition PBK 9 8 7 6 5 4 3 2 1

Table of Contents

The first vampire appeared in a Greek story more than 2,000 years ago. Vampires are creatures that can live forever. They drink blood.

Most vampires are said to drink human blood, but some drink animal blood.

The word vampire comes from a Greek word meaning "to drink."

Vampires bite people.
These victims might then turn into vampires. But vampires need human helpers, too. A vampire can **hypnotize** its helper. This person will keep the vampire safe while it sleeps.

hypnotize to place a person in a sleep-like state during which their thoughts and actions are easily influenced

Early vampires were called upyr (*OOP-air*). This means "undead." The vukodlak (*VOO-cud-lac*) is related to the vampire. It eats people's hearts during a full moon. The jiangshi is a vampire in Chinese **folklore**. This creature moves stiffly.

folklore traditional beliefs, stories, or customs that are passed on by word of mouth

Sleeping in coffins keeps vampires from burning in sunlight.

Vampires can be found in all countries. Some are part of groups led by rulers. Some make their homes in dark castles. Others roam **cemeteries**. Vampires may sleep in **coffins** during the day.

cemeteries graveyards; places where dead people are buried

coffins boxes to hold dead bodies for burial

Some stories say vampires are shapeshifters. They can turn into bats or wolves. They can become mist or shadows. This may be how vampires follow their victims.

Vampires may be able to change into bats, owls, rats, or wolves.

Vampires can smell when other vampires are near. They may hunt together. Vampires can see distant objects and hear weak sounds. They can control animals, fire, and water with their thoughts.

Vampires' sharp senses help them find victims and avoid hunters.

Holy places cause vampires pain.
They stay away from churches. Vampires also avoid mirrors. They do not have a reflection. A sharp piece of wood through the heart will destroy a vampire.

A sharpened piece of wood used to destroy vampires is known as a stake.

Though many otherkins are harmless creatures, some play tricks on humans.

Vampires are part of otherkin **culture**. Most otherkins are beings that are partly human. This group also includes angels, demons, fairies, and more.

culture beliefs and behaviors shared by a group

Today, vampires are stars of books, movies, and television shows. They are not always evil. Some, like Count von Count on *Sesame Street*, are friendly.

The friendly Count von Count tallies everything he sees!

A *Vampire Story*

Adhampir is the child of a vampire and a human. One dhampir's purpose in life was to hunt and destroy vampires. She could feel the energy of vampires around her. She could track them to their hiding places. Like all dhampirs, she was fearless. She knew how to use many weapons. But her favorite was a wooden stake!

Read More

Klepeis, Alicia Z. *Vampires: The Truth Behind History's Creepiest Bloodsuckers*. Mankato, Minn.: Capstone Press, 2016.

Tieck, Sarah. *Vampires*. Minneapolis: ABDO, 2016.

Wilberforce, Bert. *Vampire Bats Drink Blood!* New York: Gareth Stevens, 2018.

Websites

CBC Kids: Eight Spooky Things You Might Know About Vampires
https://www.cbc.ca/kidscbc2/the-feed/monsters-101-all-about-vampires
Read more facts about mysterious vampires.

Mocomi Kids: Vampire Facts and History
https://youtu.be/bLDSU5hxGrM
Watch a short video to learn more about vampires.

Note: Every effort has been made to ensure that the websites listed above are suitable for children, that they have educational value, and that they contain no inappropriate material. However, because of the nature of the Internet, it is impossible to guarantee that these sites will remain active indefinitely or that their contents will not be altered.